AQUEOUS RED

C000085498

Kit Ingram is a prize-winning queer Canadian poet, writer, and editor based in London. His work has been widely anthologised and appeared in *Ambit*, *Magma*, and *The North*. His narrative poem, *Alice and Antius* (Penrose Press, 2022) was a *Booklife at Publishers Weekly* selection described as a 'moving, gorgeous novel in verse … and must-read elegy for the Anthropocene.' *Aqueous Red* is his debut UK collection of poetry. More at: https://kitingram.com / @kitingramwrites

Also by Kit Ingram

Alice and Antius	(Penrose Press, 2022)
Paradise	(Ganymede Press, 2021)

Aqueous Red

Kit Ingram

Broken Sleep Books

ISBN: 978-1-915760-40-1

Cover designed by Aaron Kent

Edited and Typeset by Aaron Kent

Broken Sleep Books Ltd
Rhydwen
Talgarreg
Ceredigion
SA44 4HB

Broken Sleep Books Ltd
Fair View
St Georges Road
Cornwall
PL26 7YH

Contents

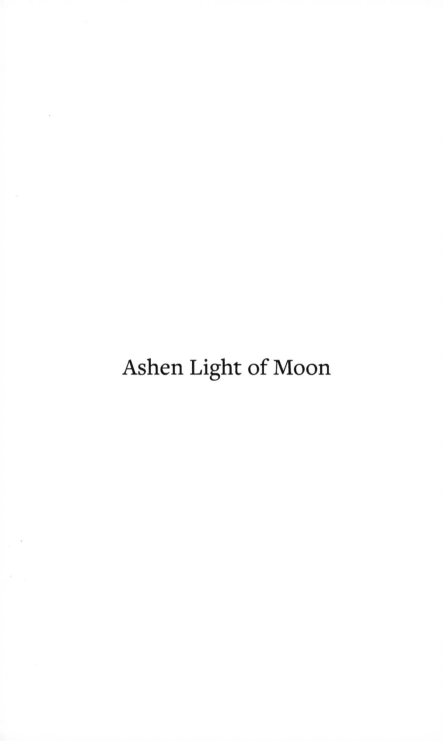

Ashen Light of Moon

Bones and other bits of architecture
crack and buckle. He collapses,
reaches for the Bombay Sapphire ('Sunset' edition)
empty – *whoosh* – he drank it
as the moon watched, its eye
half blackened by night,
then blued by a noon sky
ringing with birds. He craves morning,

the robins and thrushes trilling
before the sun heaves over the horizon.
He's no misanthrope,
but his hate grows when
the arguing through the walls of this terraced house
spikes his anxiety. Maybe he's the cause.
Hence the audio punishments,
The Piper at the Gates of Dawn
blaring ad infinitum.

Once, before
he stopped talking to strangers,
he met the gardener
sawing the hands off the neighbours' tree.
She asked if she could clear the debris from his yard
(her clients, actuaries
the risk, untenable)
and he said not to worry –
he'd make a sculpture of these crooked fingers
reaching up to the light.

✦

Sex workers tricked
his sleepy lane into a thoroughfare –
the Victorian cottages, a break from the greasy
adjoining streets, the warehouses sick
in the ashen light of moon.

He thought these laugh peddlers
would wait for an audience,
but they scutter
in jerky movements
as if hidden strings yank their limbs.
Sometimes a figure
will glance at his window
and mistake his palm on the pane for a wave
and not desperation for the light
of celestial bodies. He worries
about vitamin D deficiency,

so pops tablets from the blister pack,
chases them down with milk. Something obscene
about all the choking. He'd rather die
with gin on his lips, an assassin's ghost
sliding over him with a silenced gun.

✦

Sometimes pushed down
the stairs by a laughing child
or chained to a rock,
his organs beaked out by an eagle
with cold gold eyes.

Other times falling, snapping through branches
and landing teeth-down in a lake,
which turns out to be a puddle.
He rises, mute
reaching
for the succubus who left him
when he started drinking before noon
and accusing the faces on Zoom
of imprisoning
him, the moon, a peeled lychee

in the deep water –
how light shrinks from the surface
as the drink burns off.

He doesn't have quips
for the bullies of doom.
His parents used to squeak
inflatable water wings over his arms
and thrust him into cannonballs.
Every time he survived,
he got a treat from the shop
where they sold condoms and packets
of broken-up crisps. *Salt & Vinegar*.
The itch in his muzzle was lip-smack-
exquisite. Today, he wakes to the blessing of rain,
not his screaming.

✦

That Joni song comes on
with the line about the devil,
and he thinks of his mother's mouth
warped like a goblin
whenever she caught him
pained by the red sufferings of ungulates
on *National Geographic*.

His friend Sabrina used to capture ants
and corral them on the pavement –
cook them on a hot coin of light
and sell him the pleasure.
Her eye at the magnifying glass
drowned him in a blink.

Kids these days innovate
torture. They steal e-bikes and rage
down the pavement,
shutter-slamming,
snapping off the views of enthusiast peepers.
'Doris' is the latest and misses

when the man plays house
in his skinniest briefs. Nothing sexy –
he grinds the oranges against the juicer,
guzzles a cup. Bits tickle his throat
like shivers of glass.

✦

His eye eclipses the peephole and finds
the delivery person on the pavement,
three hours late, face bruised by shadow.
Issue with the melons, they say, and lift a full moon
from a paper bag,
inspecting its dark side for craters.
This vendor is never on time! they crow.
But 'always' and 'never' are words

he categorically rejects –
Truths flicker! Consider old Schrödinger's
cat sealed in a box
with a flask of radionuclides.
Quantum mechanics says
the feline is alive
or dead.
The absurdity of thought
experiments! He imagines many things
but not contravening

the laws of the universe:

splash gin over ice
until crackles
sound alive
while always dying.

TRIPTYCH

I

He speaks to the water / In the third-floor lavatory of the flooding gallery / he lowers his lips to the basin / It listens / renders his messages in tongues no one can untangle / The louder his secrets / the safer it keeps them / When he stops / the reflection stirs to a blur / eyes trembling like a room in translation / Now another man is staring at him / melting / necktie hanging like a flap of skin / a clue of red cloud / diffusing through the water in a drunken sunset / He tries to walk out of this strange life / and slips into a mirror

II

A skull missing from the body of an unnamed man /
Every night he sinks in the quiet / waiting till the darkness
squeezes him into scenes he can never escape from / rooms in
old homes visited by everyday ghosts / His father rocks
in an armchair with the cleaner kneeling between his legs /
praying / inaudibly / eyes turned glass / while in the next room
a woman is holding the telephone with the low drone
of the sea in her ear / Somewhere down the corridor / the
red man is trying to run away / but his legs are caught
in the tenderness of water / The house will hang him
on the walls like another still life / They'll never find him now

III

There he is / hauling the boy out of the river and lighting up his eyes again / *I'm sorry it took you and not me* / *Love is a junkyard of toys* / *This is a dream* / *of course* / *so you need to go back when it's over* / *Till then* / *I'll carry you like a wound* / And they pass through the trees / filling each other's lips with the same blood memories / At the bridge / they spill into a pop song / taken over by cannons and trumpets till the light rises / and the boy / falling in another war / is taken by the red water / brushed to the sea

AQUEOUS

30 Fragments

He crashes
            through the surface

in a disco   of light

            The others miss
            that he's humming

            sweet as a love song
his fingers puckered

as he turns them over
            waves to the shore

Two fathers squint at the boy
from behind their glasses

Parasols
black as Victoriana
            rattle on the beach
            a rhythm
of shells and bone

The sea's intonations follow
a history of violence
broken by idols and gods

The boy feels
        his back for fins

His father says
they were born to swim
and yet
the early motions
seem alien
far too safe with these hands
suckered to his legs

You can let go   says the boy
        and he flutters off
        thrashing the sea
        into sequins of night

All week
the roof sheds rain
into a line of pails

      some   star-filled
      others   dark
and rising with monsters

      In the morning
the man undresses and sees
        his nakedness caught
        with tails
        and claws

The bonier of the boys

drags his finger
down the glass
leaving a gash
in the steam
for his brother
to peer through

A man   darkened by rain
scrapes the innocence
from a fish

The river flails
            its white knuckles

into a misted dawn
and the air   bruised
in reds and oranges

swells to the edge
the shallows
where the boy cries
at the feet
                of a god

The neighbour spies
            from his glass hut

how the gulls' eyes pivot
from the bucket of heads

to the bloom
of the little boy's thumb
            through the tide

The wound
must be
cleansed
of debris

He takes
the boy's hand
holds it
to his cheek

He confesses   in the end
to injuries by water

How he watched
        cells burst open
as they froze
        and the scalds
        on their hands ripen
        like cherries
How liars
        in their   doggedness
drown in questions

He turns over his hands
        admires the glisten

They say blood
is predominantly water
and yet

        it thickens when dry
        leaves a kiss for
                forensics

The Atlantic
froths over
shrouds
of seaweed
An officer
claims
two bodies
of unknown
origin
washed up
tongues
bitumen black
On further
inspection
their insides
are stuffed
with scrolls
from lost sea
bottles
prayers
on some
and one
with a song
in a minor key

Skimmed a boot
from the mouth of the river
he says

then hurls it upwards
       the dried mud
       falling
       like teeth
       and the daughter
       kneeling
       to read
       their fortune

Tears of ice
                continents float
the skeletons of history

                Disembodied
                        dreams

drifting

                one
world

                to the next

Radical crow

        schemes
        over a
        mirrored
        sky
watches   the swans of
        altocumulus
        the lovers
        innocent in
        the eye of
the storm

They cling
        to a floating door

The first rhythm
        was the undulant sea

        She will wait for us
        he says

Her patience   is endless

We must keep
     our chests above water

What can freeze
     can thaw again

     Lift your ruby
     from the ocean
     and feel it   *sting*

Bloodbeats
warm
       the sea
       between them

They move closer
weaving their hands
together until his lips freeze
in a kind of   sneer

His mouth
cracks open
says   *It's over*

The motifs of

water	come to him in
grief	a flood of
love	gone belly-up
	and floating under
	the searchlights
	the rain of the Andromedids
	across a November sky

His molecules
still hanging
in the North Atlantic
as a wavelet
a plash
against this
floundering boat
She paddles
to where
the plane went down
and imagines not
radio chatter
but a shanty
a whale's song

A shadow
slides in
from under the door

and while she knows
nothing of this   her sleep
is interrupted by subtle

movements
the penetration of waves
her eye bobbing
for meaning

           in a sky
        of inkblots

Everywhere love

enciphers pain

into water

The orchids

in the conservatory

barely scream

when he shears

their roots

pins them

on the wall to dry

Gulls shatter
from the sky and land
on the clifftops

        a riotous audience

Below   sweat jitters
on the temple

        of the silken man who

        tipping the jug
cleanses the spirit

of the infant   invites us
burned and disconsolate

        to jump
           in the sea

I've swum in the
unconscious where images
of heroes
villains
and burning gardens
hiss into quiet
and the darkness
tightens

— Reverend O'Toole

He lays out the sacraments
on an altar
thrown in velvet

      This is the eye
      of a lost doll that
      sees the future

These   the stones
that brought her
to the bottom

and there   the shell
that listens back

a chalice filled with salt

The rain drips
black   down her cheeks

She stops
in the crimson glow
        and watches

the Reverend pull a vial
        from his pocket

I will sprinkle water upon you
and you shall be clean

She wakes to a mourning
a moon
           at the door

Every midnight
        is a new drowning
Will he wake
        from the moonshine
or like his mother
        slip into the river
        and turn up
        as a fist at the door
        a tongue through
        a broken
        smile

The boy rescues

         his doll

from the bottom of the tub
and presses
their lips together

I'll protect you from every
father who tries to kill you
with a grin on his face
I will brush your hair
into a beam

         of moonlight

At low tide
            the boys whisper
over pockets of mud
            and pick their prizes

a photo
            of a drag queen
with the sceptre
            of her empire

            and a skull
smoothed of its wig

a pair of coins blinking
                        in its sockets

She floods the earth
from his hair

> sweeps it to one side
> as he wore it
> when he counted
> his age in fingers
> and chased the tale
> of the sea monster

away   with a laugh

Through fathoms
of marble faces
mouths open to spheres
of glass

       the music
       of sunken lamps

the secrets of waves
the stories of bodies
lost to violence

       to gods
       and illicit liaisons
       but remembered

       by water

MY OTHER HALF MADE OF FLAME

I

In the time it takes the ammonite to unbury itself / & the
blackbird to desiccate in the wind of the dryer vent / the engine
lighting my cells rattles out / restarts / chugs me into a teenage
sprint / I'm ten miles per hour through the streets / an
unstoppable cappuccino / frothing red / Entropy is the base
code of my other identity / I could blur like pornography or
collide into a matchstick Tudor pub & set the whole place afire

II

He took to me like life / his eyes focused by adrenaline on the
blade in my grip / as if I'd slash him into a spray of red petals
/ sweep him into the bin / Love is boring / Want to burn me
with wax? / No? / How about truth? / Take a swig of the
Balvenie / dribble gleecraft onto my scars / these artefacts
from way back when I perfected casual defiance / fireworks /
skipping class / interrupting the inappropriate touching with
jagged gasps / as fault lines split to a lyric of collared doves

III

Teasing my ligaments / unrolling my tongue in the sibilance of a secret pact / our elements multiplying in refracted fires that dazzle on the inner walls / fly across the pillows like cigarette light / You were a tingle then the animating principle of my knuckles hitting the boy's orbital bone / I was jonesing to eject into the pure decadence of *float* / but we collided into a blue straggler / the twinkling chameleon scooping me into another irreducible I

RED

A BARGAIN
WITH THE GOD OF LOVE

Give us a moment & we'll give you a wound.

I

Say desire isn't a drug,
that it won't burn me in a flash of dopamine
like that afternoon you slid into the bar.

A scent dangling, faint as a dressing room emptied of roses.

I meant to charm you with an offer
of wine, something to open a heart, a skull,
an idea deep enough to lose us for a night.

Now, I spend my darkness
trying to forget you in passing windows.
The views are dizzying in a tourist city.

I always hated a happy ending, so I've taken to writing poems.
A few of them seem true, & the rest I throw to the fire,
where they flee into a sky, injured by gods.

II

Galaxies swirl on the walls
of a place named Heaven

or Paradise. The drink special is gin
with sparkling wine & a drop of bitter orange.
I order two or three
& align them like synastry.

What to make of this stranger's hand on the counter,
so perfect, the strobe light fuzzed
on the fingers like numinous filaments.

Please, don't accept my payment
without offering a number. One coffee, one walk, one minute
in a photo booth where we pose like surgical instruments
in the theatre glow.

You say you're an actor in a little play.
Same old, same old, the ending is –

tragic. What is this ring on the inside of the glass?
Will it chip into pieces,
leave a residue?
Will it shriek when I hold it to the light?

You disappear
into the backroom,
& the music peals
into stars.

III

I find your face
in the programme of the doomed
Novello Theatre.

SHAKESPEARE IN DRAG
CRESSIDA'S WRATH

That black & white thumbnail concealing
your eyes, blue as a noble gas burning with mercury.

Neon slinks into a puddle at my feet.
The doors swing open to a better world.
I see you wash in applause,
spilling your pockets at the end for a shot
glass filled with anaesthetic.

Anything could happen
if you let me in. The curtains could rise to another play.
We could be strangers in each other's bodies.

IV

Night sweeps down
the alley, traps me in a boozy flow.
People queue & chatter in vivid distractions.
Bubbles for the interval.

I search the high windows,
imagine you threading your monologue lines
through a room of sequined stars.

I remember the sound of your voice
in the light, how you smiled, & the lyrics writhed
in the close of your lips. What is a mouth but a darkness opening
to a story of marble & blood?
My ticket leads me to the edge of antiquity,
a sky in crimson silk.

This could be Troy
where the heroes die.
This could be the price of the show.

V

I'm anonymous in the pop
of camera flashes.

Girls flap programmes,
shouting proposals.

Hope he comes out
in his costume, they say.

I blink to the shades, the boots, the nude abdominals.

The flag of a ruined kingdom
hung on his shoulders.

Here he is, alarmingly
nimble in cherry red pumps.

A *she* like any other.

Each clack between autographs pierces a heart.

I wave at myself
in her silvery lenses.

The crowd disperses,
& our shadows meet.

Props can be lethal, she says,
pouting her lips.

VI

Some things happen
effortlessly – we settle your rate in the elevator,
then the room catches fire as our bodies scrape.

We can't save the clock.
Like everything else, it reduces to a question
of its own philosophy, these hands' irretrievable motions.

If you press your tongue to my mouth, you'll taste
questions, swishing over embers.
How does it end?
We burn, as every illicit word, on the altar

of silence. Don't worry; it'll only hurt
until the pain adores you.
Enter the smell, the fear & pheromones,
a dose of incense to remind us of our holiness.

I've prayed at stranger places than the ankles of a boy
with a queen inside.

VII

Plunge your thumb into my mouth.
Stopper the wine, but the words still froth over my neck
in a bliss of defiance.

I'm more delicate than I care to admit –
a gift, anyway, when you realise your earthliness.

Worship comes with a price:
Flowers after the show, a bottle of fizz to cleanse
the memory of shape-shifting gods becoming our downfall.
Are you so different with your soldier's garb,
taped-up sword, & feathered helmet?
If you keep my secret, I'll promise to

listen. We know what happens in the morning
when we sort our limbs from our words,
twist them into meaning.

                                        The light shines
                                        its own kind
                                        of violence.

VIII

You vanish into a dawn
swollen by the night's excesses.

Look.
It could be a backdrop for a West End play,
but don't mistake it for make-believe.

Look closer.
The clouds are real.
The actors dream by their own devices.
Beyond the curtains, a man is knocking on the door,

looking
to die.

Guess who?
I'm holding a fist of roses,
& you're lifting a heel as you lean in to taste them.
You shouldn't be here, you say in a radiant whisper.

Who am I but a shadow to a light,
an echo to a silence?
A wardrobe assistant smears on your heart
from an unmarked tube.

Be careful, she says.

IX

The hearts of roses sway indiscriminately.
You're tucked into a fold of shadow, smiling
like a switchblade.

We nod a greeting & follow the clicks of a man's cane
along the wiles of the Serpentine.
Little boats chug with gossip on the water.

An actor's mind never aches with questions
about the lives of the audience,
so I light a cigarette while the sun indulges
in mirrorless reflections.

You tell me your portrait is hanging in the gallery at the end,
how the label writes you into the stories of stage
& song & untimely death.

These art lovers always want to be moved, you say,
& like every mob they never give me space
to breathe.

Can I see you again? I'm back in the city next week?

Yes, you know where to find me.
I'll be glittering through the tragedies,
one song at a time.

X

Some word association?

me	you
me	**you**
smoke	*drag*
theatre	*illusion*
chocolate	*poison*
flowers	*dozens*
funerals	*magic*
romance	*satire*
secret	*crypto*
lover	*agony*
longing	*pity*
power	*dominance*
pain	*exquisite*
happiness	*bondage*

XI

Waiting for a thrill
in a suite at the unmarked hotel.
The windows are painted grey & chip away
to a glow from the American diner.

I put on the radio, & we listen
to another god, narrating a drama.
You giggle at the plot
twists in gilded bubbles. A minute later,
you're born from the jacuzzi in the middle of the room.
More Troilus than Cressida, this time around.

If I smoke, will you bloom into a marble,
tap your fingers on the ledge of the tub?
You lie back, & I break my hand
through the water, searching for proof or power
or an idol to bind you to.
I've held onto less & made it

last. I confess
to images that would shock the programmes.
Every mask-wearer knows the darkness of invention.
Let's pretend the walls aren't melting around us,
that it's only our cake, knocking
at the door.

XII

Not every image shines
by its own truth. A secret can illuminate.

Hang a gilt frame in the doorway & find a wife
crying, a view of the park in Richmond,
jewelled in green. Spin a mirror ball & see a drag queen
drawing her lips into a bow, pulling them
into a deadly smile.

I have to get home, you say.
Mum always stays awake until
she hears my last drink clinking down the hallway.

Wait.
Give me a morning, & I'll give you a face
of inimical light, your eye squinting to find me
a word's length away. You never asked my name.
I call you Billie, & you beam like every other arrow
cushioned by a heart.

XIII

The afternoon reddens
while I wait for you at the edge of the Heath.
We could be tumbling in a room
with the shadows of Plato,
if you didn't laugh at that sort of thing.

I fray between oaks,
charged by the wind, rasping
through the trees,
the gambling crows overhead.
They know what's coming. Autumn's redware
shatters along the field like the fury

of history. I used to paint over there, enslaved
by dimensions that could never hold the scenes.
Men surfaced from the water, dripping with pondweed
& fled in the captive sun.

I'd heard this place whispered about
in the stone heart of the City.
The darkness, where you find it, is lush with desires,
light-footed as tricksters
or thieves. You never know they're coming
until they blind you with fingers
& make you hand over their names.

We play the guessing game that ends with skin
transfigured by the scores of branches.
Ecstasy, as you like to say.

XIV

Don't leave.

For every pain we free in each other,
I wonder if there isn't a small corner where a boy
huddles. He could be tucked in the attic,
where the roar of slamming doors is lost
in a history of unopened boxes.
Inside, he finds every smile
sunk in the darkness of his father's eye,
every missing toy he explained away
with his own carelessness
when his parents had taken them,
dropped them in unmarked graves.

Near the bottom, blurred in shadow,
he finds the belt he wore in his Year One photo,
the belt his father had notched for him
across every vertebra
when he'd found the boy playing
make-believe with his sister's dolls & dresses.

I knew that boy. He lived
in our village,
in every tourist town we visited,
in my house, though no one knew until he left.
He said he was never coming back.

XV

I find you floating over the mattress,
your breath fitful as a dreaming flame.
The moon deciphers the skin
of your eyelids, prickling with questions, critics
to escape before the morning ruins us with meaning.

This is our room for the night,
puddled in red feathers & singing with emergencies.
London is always burning.
If it wasn't the theatre crackling with applause,
it would be the stories of forbidden lovers.

I melt my skin into your shape, pour around you,
gentle as cooling wax, sealed from trespass.
I never expected more than this fantasy to wrap around
as the buildings ring with fire, as the smoke
whispers under the doors & tells us
this is the end & the beginning.

We must wake up. We must never
surrender these bodies to the light.

XVI

We wake up, of course we do,
& it's snowing
as the burned-out streets of Soho crunch
under our steps.

I take you to the diner
where the clown in goth's clothing delivers us
the Daily Specials between lines of the Bard.
Turns out, he's a castmate of yours, an understudy,
waiting for his big break.

He asks if I'm your father, honking at his own joke,
& you say I'm the director of a new play
you're starring in, an Off West End romp through taboos
with original music by a 'Sir' so-and-so.
I get lost in all this, reminiscing
through the photos of strangers on the walls,
lives hypnotic as the lies we tell ourselves.

I ask if they have cherry pie
made with real cherries, not those sweet baubles
hanging on the tree in the window.

The silence falls like the sky, building
until it blows into an eddy. *I need a break,* you say.
I'm leaving for an island where the play never ends.
The forecast is always sunny.

XVII

I could finish us off with a call to my wife. A kinky ending, if a little easy. Instead, I dream into a room where you flow in a moon-red gown & ask if I'll help read through lines from the final act. The stars are scorching through the window – the bed, another relic with its scripts & handcuffs. Before we ever get to the play, a god interrupts with an emergency broadcast. Two voices, unnamed, banter in questions:

Is it different than obsession?

> *Must we hold it in one hand,*
> *or can we share it?*

Will the wind & the words
that carry it, kill it, too?

> *What drew you to her?*
> *The cracks shone through*
> *with sadness?*

Is there a secret
holding it together?

> *How long until the heart tires*
> *& the imagination*
> *takes over?*

What if time regresses
to a single red moment?

What if love is a contract
that must be broken for us
to make sense of it?

[A chorus of static]

You turn in the light of a day, closing behind bolt & key.
Knock before, you say, & like all the other dreams,
I'm devastated by the memory of time.

I could wake to a morning disfigured by bus schedules,
the racket of twigs snapping on the height of our double-decker.
You'll pass me a screen with a video of an MTV pop queen singing
about standing still in time, as if we hadn't tried with gin poured over
ice in that bar called Heaven.

I'd rather wake to the adrenaline of sun on water, the boat
waiting at the end of the dock for our row into the middle of
a summer before the air got too risky to breathe. Like now.
My heart dialled up, a base line fast-forwarding to a lyricless hum
through the door, our bodies, shadow on shadow, pressed into
bondage.

Every secret is a hole opened by a flick of tongues against silence.
Let's break into the unspeakable & forget these hours, these
sweeping hands, one last time.

Acknowledgements

Thank you to the judges of the National Poetry Competition, the Bridport Prize, and the Out-Spoken Prize for Poetry for recognising earlier versions of these poems.

Thank you to Cher Li, whose care, insights, and friendship have made my creative life less lonely. And thank you to my fellow poets for their bravery, compassion, and freewheeling minds. You inspire me every day.

Finally, thank you to Aaron Kent and the Broken Sleep team for championing diverse voices and providing a home for my first collection. I'm so proud to be part of the history of this vital press.

LAY OUT YOUR AQUEOUS UNREST